First Facts®

National Landmarks

THE LINCOLN MEMORIAL

A 4D BOOK

by Erin Edison

PEBBLE
a capstone imprint

Download the Capstone 4D app!

- Ask an adult to download the Capstone 4D app.
- Scan the cover and stars inside the book for additional content.

When you scan a spread, you'll find fun extra stuff to go with this book! You can also find these things on the web at www.capstone4D.com using the password: lincoln.31305

First Facts are published by Pebble
1710 Roe Crest Drive, North Mankato, Minnesota 56003
www.mycapstone.com

Library of Congress Cataloging-in-Publication Data

Names: Edison, Erin, author.
Title: The Lincoln Memorial : a 4D book / by Erin Edison.
Description: North Mankato, Minnesota : Pebble, 2019. | Series: First facts. National landmarks.
Identifiers: LCCN 2018004147 (print) | LCCN 2018012365 (ebook) | ISBN 9781543531381 (eBook PDF) | ISBN 9781543531305 (hardcover) | ISBN 9781543531343 (pbk.)
Subjects: LCSH: Lincoln Memorial (Washington, D.C.)—History—Juvenile literature. | Lincoln, Abraham, 1809–1865—Monuments—Washington (D.C.)—Juvenile literature. | Lincoln, Abraham, 1809–1865—Influence—Juvenile literature. | Washington (D.C.)—Buildings, structures, etc.—Juvenile literature. Classification: LCC F203.4.L73 (ebook) | LCC F203.4.L73 E35 2019 (print) | DDC 975.3—dc23
LC record available at https://lccn.loc.gov/2018004147

Editorial Credits

Erika L. Shores, editor; Sarah Bennett, designer; Eric Gohl, media researcher; Tori Abraham, production specialist

Photo Credits

Getty Images: George Rinhart, 17, Library of Congress, 14, 19; Library of Congress: 7, 8, 9, 11, 13 (bottom), 18; Newscom: UPI Photo Service, 20; Shutterstock: ETIENjones, 5 (bottom), Everett Historical, 10, jiawangkun, 15, Kamira, 5 (top), Orhan Cam, cover, PSboom, 4, S.Borisov, 21; Wikimedia: Public Domain, 13 (top)

Design Elements: Shutterstock

Table of Contents

A National Landmark

The Lincoln Memorial is a **symbol** of freedom. Every year more than 7 million people visit the memorial in Washington, D.C. They remember Abraham Lincoln and the work he did for the United States.

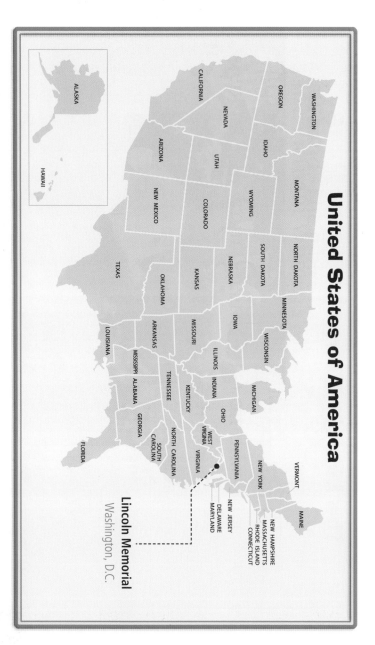

United States of America

Lincoln Memorial
Washington, D.C.

Visitors from all over the world come to see the Lincoln Memorial (above). A giant statue of Lincoln (right) is inside the building.

symbol—an object that reminds people of something else

About Abraham Lincoln

Abraham Lincoln became president on March 4, 1861. In April the Civil War started between the northern and the southern states. The South wanted strong state governments. The North wanted a strong **federal** government. The South also wanted slavery to stay **legal**. But many people in the North thought slavery was wrong.

federal—the central government

legal—allowed by the rules

Abraham Lincoln

Lincoln worked to keep the nation together. He thought people should be free and equal. In 1863 he signed the **Emancipation Proclamation**. This law said slaves in the South were free.

Lincoln (third from left) showed the proclamation to members of his cabinet before it became law.

Emancipation Proclamation—a document signed by President Abraham Lincoln, which freed slaves

A copy of the Emancipation Proclamation

The Civil War ended in April 1865. The United States remained together as one country. Some people had not liked Lincoln's ideas. On April 14, John Wilkes Booth shot Lincoln. Lincoln died the next morning.

Booth jumped from a balcony after he shot President Lincoln.

People lined a New York City street to watch Lincoln's coffin pass by on the way to his funeral.

Honoring a President

People wanted to honor Lincoln.
In 1911 Congress set up the Lincoln
Memorial **Commission.**

Pierre Charles L'Enfant had designed
Washington. He planned a long, grassy
mall. This big park would have trees and
monuments. The Capitol Building sat at
the east end of the Mall. The commission
thought a grand building at the west end
would be perfect.

commission—a group of people who meet
to solve a problem or do certain tasks

This 1912 photograph shows the area before the memorial was built.

Members of the Lincoln Memorial Commission

Planning a Monument

Architect Henry Bacon designed the memorial. He modeled it after a famous Greek building called the Parthenon. Bacon included 36 **columns** around the outside of the building. They stand for the 36 states in the country when Lincoln died. The names of 48 states are above the columns.

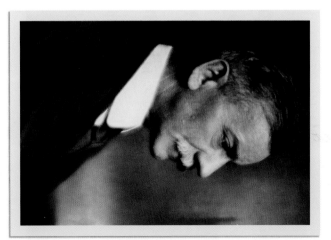

Henry Bacon

architect—a person who designs and draws plans for buildings, bridges, and other construction projects

column—a tall, upright post that helps support a building or statue

FACT

The country had 48 states when the memorial was completed. Later a sign was added to include Alaska and Hawaii.

Bacon planned three rooms for the monument. The center room has a statue of Lincoln. The other rooms include Lincoln's speeches. The commission chose the Second **Inaugural Address** and the Gettysburg Address. Lincoln gave this famous speech on November 19, 1863, in Gettysburg, Pennsylvania. He said the government should be run by the people and for the people.

FACT

Sculptor Daniel Chester French designed the 19-foot (6-meter) tall statue of Lincoln. The statue is made out of marble.

Inaugural Address—the speech the president gives when sworn into office

Daniel Chester French was the sculptor of the Lincoln statue.

The Lincoln Memorial

Work on the memorial started in 1914. It opened to visitors on May 30, 1922. This date was about 57 years after Lincoln died. At least 50,000 people came to honor Lincoln. Thousands more people listened to the speeches on radios in their homes.

This photograph shows the outside of the memorial being built.

A huge crowd gathered to view the opening of the Lincoln Memorial in 1922.

People gather at the Lincoln Memorial for many events. In 1963 as many as 250,000 people came to Washington, D.C. They wanted the government to pass a **civil rights bill.** Dr. Martin Luther King Jr. gave his famous "I Have a Dream" speech at the memorial. He said everyone should have equal rights.

civil rights bill—a law that said all people should be treated equally

Dr. Martin Luther King Jr. waved to the crowd at the Lincoln Memorial in 1963.

About the Lincoln Memorial

Height: 99 feet (30 m)

Width: 120 feet (37 m)

Length: 190 feet (58 m)

Construction material: marble

Cost in 1922: about $3 million

Glossary

architect (AR-ki-tekt)—a person who designs and draws plans for buildings, bridges, and other construction projects

civil rights bill (SI-vil RYTS BIL)—a law that said all people should be treated equally

column (KAH-luhm)—a tall, upright post that helps support a building or statue

commission (kuh-MISH-uhn)—a group of people who meet to solve a problem or do certain tasks

Emancipation Proclamation (i-MAN-si-pay-shuhn prah-cluh-MAY-shuhn)—a document signed by President Abraham Lincoln, which freed slaves

federal (FED-ur-uhl)—the central government

Inaugural Address (in-AW-ger-ul ad-DRESS)—the speech the president gives when sworn into office

legal (LEE-guhl)—allowed by the rules

symbol (SIM-buhl)—an object that reminds people of something else

Read More

Duling, Kaitlyn. *Lincoln Memorial.* Hello, America! Minneapolis: Jump!, Inc., 2017.

Kirkman, Marissa. *The Life and Times of Abraham Lincoln and the U.S. Civil War.* First Facts: Life and Times. North Mankato, Minn.: Capstone Press, 2017.

Kissock, Heather, ed. *Lincoln Memorial.* Symbols of America. New York: Smartbook Media Inc., 2017.

Internet Sites

Use FactHound to find Internet sites related to this book.

Visit *www.facthound.com*

Just type in 9781543531305 and go.

Super-cool stuff!

Check out projects, games and lots more at **www.capstonekids.com**

Critical Thinking Questions

1. Why did some people disagree with Lincoln's ideas during his lifetime?

2. Describe two important parts of the Lincoln Memorial and what they stand for.

3. Why was the Lincoln Memorial a good place to hold a march for civil rights?

Index